S0-ANN-543

Finally, there's a way to learn how to divine your very own future in love. For several hundred years, people have consulted with Tarot readers on the subjects of life and love. When it comes to matters of the heart, readers skilled in the art of Tarot are able to interpret the way you pick your cards, and advise you on your destiny. This reference book takes you through the meaning, reading and interpretation of the cards. Let the 78 cards show you and your friends the ways of love, sex and choosing - or losing - a partner. Learn all about the meanings behind the Tarot of Love cards, and the ways in which you can benefit from their use.

Keren Lewis was born in Italy. She saw the Tarot skills of her mother and grandmother displayed at home, as friends and neighbors had their cards spread and read. Lewis moved to New York City where she continued to share the wisdom derived from reading Tarot cards. She specializes in the subjects of love, sex and choosing the right partner as determined by the cards. This is her first book.

LITTLE **BIG** BOOK SERIES:

Basic Numerology
by Lia Robin

Bach Flower Remedies
by David Lord

Dream Interpretation
by Eili Goldberg

I Ching
by Nizan Weisman

The Tarot of Love
by Keren Lewis

Basic Palmistry
by Batia Shorek

Aura:
Understanding, Seeing and Healing
by Connie Islin

The Zodiac: A Year of Signs
by Amanda Starr

Crystals and Stones
by Connie Islin

Chakras
by Lily Rooman

Tarot
by Keren Lewis

Runes
by Hali Morag

LITTLE BIG BOOK

of

the Tarot
of Love

by Keren Lewis

Astrolog Publishing House

Astrolog Publishing House
P.O. Box 1123, Hod Hasharon 45111, Israel
Tel: 972-9-7412044
Fax: 972-9-7442714
E-Mail: info@astrolog.co.il
Astrolog Web Site: www.astrolog.co.il

© Keren Lewis 1998

ISBN 965-494-055-8

All rights reserved. No part of this publication may be
reproduced, stored in a retrieval system, or transmitted in
any form or by any means, electronic, mechanical,
photocopying, recording or otherwise, without the prior
permission of the publisher.
Illustrations from the Rider-Waite Tarot Deck®.
Reproduced by permission of U.S. Games
Systems, Inc., Stamford, CT 06902 USA.
Copyright© 1971 by U.S. Games Systems, Inc.

Published by Astrolog Publishing House 1998

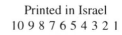

Printed in Israel
10 9 8 7 6 5 4 3 2 1

INTRODUCTION

Professional card readers know that most of the questions that arise during a spread of the cards concern the relationships between the sexes, problems related to love or the search for perfect love. Over the years, therefore, an entire approach has developed, one dedicated solely to interpreting the cards with regard to love - and this is the one used by Tarot readers.

One does not require a special deck of cards in order to spread and interpret the Tarot of Love. Any pack containing the 78 tarot cards is suitable, and any Tarot card may be transformed, with the aid of the appropriate interpretation, into a Tarot of Love card. There are, however, special decks for the Tarot of Love, and the cards in these decks are illustrated in a manner depicting the different aspects of love.

Similarly, the usual spreads associated with the Tarot will be used, but the interpretation will be directed toward the relevant area.

In the Tarot of Love, the Tarot deck is divided into two sets: The 22 cards of the *Major Arcana*, which provide general trends, tendencies and problems; and the 56 cards of the *Lesser*

Arcana (including the Knight cards) which go into details and highlight unique and special issues relating to the querent (the person for whom the cards are being read).

When reading the Tarot of Love, the choice of the *Significator Card* is very important in a spread which requires such a representative card. It is crucial to choose the Significator Card correctly, according to the querent and following the criteria below:

First, we choose one of the minor suits according to the querent's birth date (age), in coordination with the astrological Sun Sign, following the accepted rules. (The Significator Card is chosen from among a selection of cards from the Lesser Arcana containing four suits: Swords, Wands, Cups and Pentacles.)

The Swords suit for Libra, Gemini and Aquarius (the air signs)
The Wands suit for Aries, Leo and Sagittarius (the fire signs)
The Cups suit for Cancer, Scorpio and Pisces (the water signs)
The Pentacles suit for Taurus, Virgo and Capricorn (the earth signs)

One of the court cards (King, Queen, Knight, Page) is selected from the appropriate suit, according to the following rule:

For a man under the age of 40: **Knight**
For a man over the age of 40: **King**
For a woman under the age of 40: **Page**
For a woman over the age of 40: **Queen**

In the Tarot of Love, we occasionally use other names for the court cards:

King is called **Man**.
Queen is called **Woman**.
Knight is called **Prince**.
Page is called **Princess**.

In this book, we will use different names:
Prince for a man under the age of 40.
King for a man over the age of 40.
Princess for a woman under the age of 40.
Queen for a woman over the age of 40.

We will now examine the interpretations of the different cards, beginning with the Major Arcana.

THE MAJOR ARCANA

THE FOOL.

0 The Fool

This card is the card of illusion - "ideal" love, which does not actually exist in reality. It is the dream about the handsome prince on a white horse, or the sleeping beauty in a silent castle.

When this card appears in a spread concerning love, it is very meaningful. It testifies to the fact that the querent yearns for an ideal, perfect love, and the discrepancy between this longing and reality occasionally creates tension and disappointment. This holds true for both men and women.

(Some Tarot readers use this card as a Joker; in other words, it gives the querent the possibility of finding true love with *any partner*. Those querents who use their character traits in the right way will succeed in turning any love relationship into a perfect one.)

1 The Magician

This card signifies the beginning of a new relationship *for a woman*. It indicates the start of a new love relationship, a new lover, a new acquaintance. The card is charged with potent male energy which is directed mainly at the couple's sexuality.

2 The High Priestess

This card indicates love originating from a spiritual source. It is most significant for *a man:* a strong female influence en route to true love, and meeting a loving woman with a strong personality.

3 The Empress

This card has a double meaning. On the one hand, it shows a strong relationship that the querent has with a mother figure - he is searching for, or wants to imagine, a mother who, over the years, acquires the nature of a "saint".

On the other hand, regarding the querent himself, it speaks of a serious, mature partner with whom a fruitful and long-lasting relationship will develop.

(The image of the mother is related to fertility and childbirth.)

4 The Emperor

This card, like the Empress card, also has a double meaning. On the one hand, it testifies to a strong relationship that the querent has with a father figure. The father acquires the image of protector and patron.

On the other hand, when this card is reversed, it may indicate residual sexual traumas caused by the father during childhood (but it does not refer to incest or sexual abuse).

Regarding the querent himself, the card indicates a stable, established and long-lasting love relationship, in accordance with legal and accepted norms.

5 The Hierophant

This is a spiritual card, one which is linked to true love. Actually, the appearance of this card indicates that the querent's love will only be fully expressed within the normative framework of the society in which he lives.

It is an important card especially for those with a strict religious lifestyle. This card overshadows an entire spread whenever it appears.

6 The Lovers

What more can be said! This card indicates full sexual arousal, total eroticism, without which love is not complete. Usually, this card refers to a *new* love, but, depending on the adjacent cards in the spread, there is a possibility of a rekindling of an existing or old love.

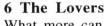

7 The Chariot

This is a difficult card in terms of pure love. It indicates that the querent has a "strong friendship" with two or more friends. It is vague about the gender of the friend and may indicate, particularly when the Chariot is reversed, homosexual or lesbian love.

Usually, this friendship is also connected to sexual relations, the physical expression being more dominant than the spiritual. This card signifies problems concerning love, which results mainly from a poor self-image.

8 Strength

This card has an unmistakably sexual connotation, relating to a peak or climax (or, in the physical realm, to orgasm) which the querent may reach. If the card is upright, it indicates that a love relationship will reach its peak.

If the card is reversed, it predicts difficulties on the way to that peak.

The card focuses on a narrow aspect of love relationships and should not be underestimated.

9 The Hermit

A very significant card for the querent, as it directs him inward, toward himself.

In other words, in order for a person to be in a relationship of which the element of love is an important component, he must first love himself and be at one with himself.

This card has the same meaning whether it appears upright or reversed.

10 Wheel of Fortune

This is one of the most important cards in any spread concerning love - a new cycle of love is about to begin!

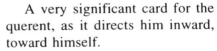

We do not know whether this is a new love, the renewal of an old love, or an existing love which is moving on to a new stage; however, we do know that the change will be significant and tangible.

Many believe that this new cycle is actually the fulfillment of an old karmic designation, and emphasize the significance of this card, particularly after a serious crisis. Upright or reversed, there is no difference in the meaning,.

11 Justice

Justice, or "Balance", is a card that indicates equilibrium in the relationship between a man and a woman - a steady relationship with a great deal of mutual respect.

When this card is reversed, it testifies to an imbalance between the two people.

The card is particularly significant for evaluating the wholeness and continuity of the relationship over time.

12 The Hanged Man

A difficult card. When this card appears in a man's spread, particularly when reversed, it indicates physical problems related to the sexual fulfillment of love.

Only rarely does a "corrective" card show up by its side, enabling the man's potency to return. When this card appears in a woman's spread (reversed or upright) it attests to numerous inhibitions and problems from her past that are interfering with her ability to attain true love at this stage of her life.

13 Death

As its name signifies, the card tells of the death of an old love... but the beginning of a new love as well! The death of the old love is strongly interconnected with the new love, and it is even a favorable sign.

In many ways, this card is similar to the Wheel of Fortune card, except that this time it focuses on a particular segment of the large circle. The time period to which this card refers will be a difficult one.

14 Temperance

An excellent card, indicating total harmony between lovers, both emotionally and physically, a balance which suits their ages according to the energy emanating from them. They will attain self-fulfillment by means of their love.

This is an important card, especially for men. When it is reversed, the harmony still exists, but to a lesser extent.

15 The Devil

This card speaks of straying from the path of true, correct love for the sake of momentary physical pleasure.

One might say that this card, whether upright or reversed, indicates that impulse has overcome rational thought, and that physical desire has dominated the querent's soul and sense of morality.

It is important to understand that this card violates the accepted frameworks of society and may therefore also be interpreted - with caution - as the betrayal of a correct love.

This is a particularly difficult card when *The Tower* appears after it.

16 The Tower

This is a difficult card. It points to a rapid, extreme change in a relationship that had once been a loving one.

It indicates divorce, infidelity, a number of sexual problems, venereal diseases... or impotence!

This is one of the most problematic cards, and it would be best if it didn't appear at all!

17 The Star

This card symbolizes new hope. It is significant when it follows a card that indicates crisis, break-up or weakening.

It testifies to the ability of the querent to repair the rupture.

(To a great extent, it resembles the square that appears on a broken line on the palm of the hand.)

This card is particularly powerful when it is upright, and less so when it appears reversed.

Its advantage lies in the fact that it "obscures" the disagreement or the momentary problem, and reveals the foundation of true love... *if true love actually exists in the querent's relationship.*

18 The Moon

This is an important card which indicates that the querent is seeking his soul-mate or predestined partner.

Its appearance means that the querent is indeed close to his most suitable partner.

19 The Sun

This card indicates love that manifests itself primarily externally, both in its physical and in its emotional aspects.

In other words, it is a love whose expression is directed towards the outer world in which the lovers live.

When this card appears, it is an indication of possible problems or cracks in a "mask" of love which, on the surface, appears to be perfect.

20 The Last Judgment

A card that demands a change in the realm of physical sexuality, particularly if reversed.

The querent must examine his sexual past, and if he is unable to cope with his problems, he must seek counseling.

21 The World

The perfect card! The querent is approaching the total; fulfillment of true love, and this fulfillment will help him realize his highest potential, in accordance with his destiny.

Naturally, if the card is reversed, the validity of the interpretation is weakened.

THE LESSER ARCANA

The Lesser Arcana of the Tarot of Love consists of four suits: Wands, Pentacles, Cups and Swords. Each of the suits contains ten cards with numerological values, ranging from 1 (Ace) to 10, and four "figure" cards or court cards: King, Queen, Prince and Princess. (Note the comment about the names in the Introduction!)

It is important to remember that in the Tarot of Love, the "court cards" or "family cards", always include all four figures. In the regular Tarot deck, the four Knight cards are sometimes separate from the others, forming a small fifth set consisting of the four Knight cards.

Each suit has spheres of "interest" that are unique to the suit. Similarly, each of the *numerological cards* (1 to 10) has a special numerological interpretation (which is identical throughout all the suits), and each of the *court cards* has its own unique meaning (also identical throughout all the suits). The sphere and the interpretation of each card are based, therefore, on the *unique and particular* interpretation of every card in the Tarot of Love.

We will begin by presenting the key words

for each of the four suits. Next, we will present the key words for the numerological and court cards. Finally, after we have become familiar with the spheres and characteristics of each card, we will discuss the interpretations of the 56 cards of the Lesser Arcana in greater detail.

Wands

This is a guiding suit by means of which the querent can find his path or grope in the dark; he can also lean on it, using it as a solid support. This suit offers him protection and guides him along an enchanted path to lofty destinations.

Key Words: Air, energy, ideals, change. Love here is idealistic, internal, spiritual – to a great extent, an intuitive love that ignores the development of one's creativity and follows the heart.

Pentacles

This suit deals with the material element, the realization of one's life. It is a suit that seeks the path of life leading to wealth, happiness and security, and in particular, great stability. It guides the querent toward those goals that are legitimate and acceptable in the society in which he lives and functions.

Key Words: Earth, possessions, constructive energy, profitable activity. Erotic love (both physical and emotional). To a great extent, this love may sweep the querent off his feet and detach him from the foundations of his life.

Cups

In the Tarot of Love, this suit is referred to as a "water" suit - soft, blending with nature. The suit teaches us how to cope with emotions, feelings and the energies between partners. This suit is particularly important with regard to fertility, continuity and eternity.

Key Words: Water, fulfillment, energy, feeling. Emotional motivation, erotic-sensual love. May indicate that the querent is "losing himself" in his emotions.

Swords

This suit teaches us about the explosive, rapid and destructive power contained in the element of fire. It speaks of the quality of speed. However, it also provides the tool to cope with danger. The Sword in the Tarot of Love is always a double-edged sword, that is, it cuts in both directions. This suit indicates an accumulation of tension... but also the orgasm of love!

Key Words: Fire, power, physical and spiritual energy. Emotional motivation. Change. Active sexuality (even in an aggressive manner). Polarity. Magnetic energy (attracting/repelling). May lead to a harmful fixation in one's love life.

Key Words for the Court Cards:

King. An opportunity to gain control over the masculine energy, the eastern Yang, or Animus. The realm of integration resulting from a collaboration between *male* and female. The father image.

Queen. An opportunity to gain control over the feminine energy, the eastern Yin, or Anima. The realm of integration resulting from a collaboration between *female* and male. The mother image.

Prince. The dominating principle, the relationship that stems from authority, looking down on others. The rising Yang powers. The "awakening" of the Animus.

Princess. The receptive principle, the relationship through merging, looking at others from within. The Yin powers are all-absorbing. The "awakening" of the Anima in order to unite with the Animus.

Key Words for the Numerological Cards:

1. (Ace). A new beginning, an awakening, an erupting, virginal energy.

2. Yin/Yang, polarity, Anima/Animus, a duel in the field of love.

3. Creation, establishment, usefulness, reaping the fruits of one's labor.

4. Power, security, defining principles, giving substance to vague feelings.

5. Communication, meditation, decision-making, a new path (or change of path).

6. Harmony, sensitivity, delight in love and sex.

7. A sharp change, searching (desperately) for a resolution or new way.

8. Wealth, prosperity, conquest and expanding energy.

9. Conclusion, fulfillment and realization, illumination, addiction.

10. Openness, ascending to a new level, determination.

Wands

1. Harmony between different energies, soul-mates coming together, spiritual, creative love. A partner who flows with the same energy waves. An opportunity for a strong and meaningful relationship.

Reverse: A breakdown in communication, an obstruction in the flow of energy.

2. Understanding the union from the uniqueness of the masculine and the feminine, Yin/Yang, as it occurs in the encounter between partners. Building sexual identity by learning. Good communication with family members. An opportunity to attain *shared* objectives with one's partner.

Reverse: An emanation of negative energy that blocks or alienates one's partner. A distortion of the couple's relationship.

3. Sharing, building together. The desire for a joint creation. (A child?) The key word is joint creativity. The couple is searching for the shared objective which will bring them closer together.

Reverse: Rejecting the joint desire, the desire to erect an emotional barrier against one's partner.

4. Fulfillment, union, physical and spiritual connection. Here the idea becomes reality. Maintaining a close-knit circle of friends. Action leading toward a common objective - building a family or... a shared orgasm! The key words are: joint action in order to attain an objective.

Reverse: Desperately seeking self-fulfillment which contradicts, at this point, the common objective. A breach between partners. Missing the moment when they could "see the stars in the sky".

5. An intellectual relationship based on love, which becomes more and more meaningful for the partners. New lines of communication. A new path for their life together. The possibility of a *shared* change in their love life.

Reverse: Embarrassment, confusion, friction between partners. A dangerous tendency to go to extremes, thus leading to a crisis.

6. Flexibility that brings harmony, illumination. A high degree of sensitivity in love relationships (for the better!). An event that will bring both partners great happiness. Harmonious energy. Delight in sex. Joint plans.

Reverse: Cracks in the harmonious energy, lack of satisfaction. Faking in sex. The couple is missing an opportunity for pure love. At times, abstinence from sex.

7. An urgent change or adjustment is necessary in the couple's love life. Interference from the outside is threatening the relationship.

Instead of one single path, the querent has two parallel options. Pressure. The possibility of mutual respect and acknowledgment between family members. Going around in circles. Promiscuity.

Reverse: Crises, separation, divorce! Disappointment in one's sex life. Impotence. Venereal disease. A difficult period, particularly in the sexual, physical realm.

8. Fulfillment and realization in *spiritual* love. The spirit rises above the material in this stage. Receptiveness to the cosmic energy of love. Happiness in the realm of the family. Harmony. The couple cooperate *externally* in a constructive and positive manner.

Reverse: The search for a spiritual "spark" is putting an end to everyday physical love. Problems can be expected.

9. A return to love or to an old way of love. Recovery from a crisis in love life or impotence. Learning new ways of love. Change through development. A relationship comprising much more than just sexuality. The partners rely on each other for support.

Reverse: Quarrels resulting from inner turmoil. Sexual incompatibility. Sexual inhibition. A time of crisis for the couple.

10. Good communication leading to sexual fusion. Physical love leading to spiritual love. Fulfillment of karmic destiny. Challenges in living together. An urgent need for change and improvement in one's sex life.

Reverse: A missed opportunity for discovering a higher level of sexuality and love. Deadlock. Sinking into despondency as a result of sexual problems.

Queen. The ability to love intuitively, based on emotions... but also a threat hanging over a present relationship, due to the actions of another woman. The mother image as a dominating and influential figure. A woman who enslaves a man to her sexuality.

(This card is most important in a woman's spread, and less so in a man's.)

Reverse: The suppression of female sexuality. A lack of consideration for the woman on the part of the man, or a lack of development of the woman's feminine aspect.

King. Physical love, the pursuit of "penetration and conquest". Rapid force... but short-lived! A new male is affecting an existing relationship. The father image is dominating and influential. An older man winning over (a younger woman) or having a negative influence on (a younger man).

A difficult card with a potential for development, creativity, sexuality and great confusion.

Reverse: Worthy ideas or ideals cannot compete with raw sexuality. The querent (either a man or a woman) is ruled by sexuality. A dangerous card which may indicate that things are getting much worse.

KNIGHT of WANDS.

Prince. If the spread is a woman's, this card indicates the search for a new love which will afford her a new field of action. If the spread is a man's, it means that he is seeking a new love which will bolster his self-image.

This card shows an age difference which plays a role in the couple's relationship. The partners should work at forging a new relationship based on sharing and creativity.

Reverse: Crisis. Inability to withstand pressures and external temptations. A discrepancy between desire and the ability to fulfill it.

PAGE ᪕ WANDS.

Princess. A fresh virginal love (not dependent on age or experience!), which opens up new horizons. The discovery or rediscovery of physical intimacy, though love will not always reach full physical expression!

Joy and delight in the near future. Restlessness and a lack of tranquillity due to racing hormones.

Reverse: A deviation from a way of life or mode of thinking is causing the querent to stumble. He is becoming disoriented, and it is likely that he will lose his way and suffer a painful fall.

Pentacles

1. Physical harmony, joint material objectives. Erotic, sensual love. A great deal of time is dedicated to joint activity.

This card indicates the physical energy necessary for building a mutual relationship. A joint material objective for the couple or family (particularly real estate). Collaboration will have pleasant results.

Reverse: A missed opportunity for development and advancement in the material realm.

2. Material love. More precisely, the search for physical love that is apparently lacking or flawed in either one or both of the partners.

This card helps dispel the fog from love. A mutual relationship with equal flows of energy in both directions. This card may also show a considerable discrepancy in the significance that each of the partners attributes to material love (although their energy may be identical).

Reverse: Crisis, separation, divorce. Conflict about material things (money), physical problems in the fulfillment of love.

3. Creative energy is forging a new foundation for the querent's life. Fulfillment. In the right context, this card may indicate pregnancy or birth. A new direction of development. Loss of virginity. A new acquaintance with a partner from a distant land.

Reverse: A missed opportunity for a deeper and more established relationship. Separation from a partner because of travel or moving house.

4. Institutionalized love with a common basis, objective and energy. Stability. Each of the partners is well placed in his family role.

Reverse: Focusing on the material at the

expense of the spirit. A marriage of convenience. Decision-making based on financial considerations rather than on love.

5. A necessary change in the querent's love life. It is important to emphasize that the change is one that takes place within the existing framework. He has many options for change and he must choose one of them which is personal and unique for him.

Reverse: Separation which stems mainly from concern about the future. ("What will happen when I get old?"... "What will happen if I fall ill?") This card indicates that the querent is not fully satisfied with the relationship in which he is involved.

6. Romance at its best! Sensuality. Harmonious and balanced love. This card promises a balance between material - full physical love - and the romantic spirit of love!

Reverse: The querent is enslaved by his love and is, to a certain extent, losing his powers of judgment because of this fact - at times, without even being aware of the situation.

7. Searching for the way. This card is particularly important when the querent is in a love relationship, since it indicates that both partners are searching for a new kind of love. There are doubts about the future. It is especially important when there is a decision to strengthen the connection between them.

Reverse: Fear of failure. This fear is a self-fulfilling prophecy, and may actually lead to the breakdown of the existing relationship.

8. A relationship which is essentially erotic. This card also indicates wealth and "space" with regard to love. (Love of luxury? A marriage of convenience?) The card shows a tenuous energetic balance but, at the same time, mutual respect between the partners.

Reverse: Waste or abuse of sexual energy in the relationship.

9. Love is being rejected in favor of other material goals. A relationship based on convenience. Under very special circumstances, this situation may actually lead to release from the bonds of the material world! This querent needs something solid to support him and feels that he is leaning on a broken crutch.

Reverse: Stagnation due to something left over from the past. Past experience prevents the development of a balanced love relationship in the future.

10. Crisis... followed by renewed union that will strengthen this relationship. From the ruins, a new edifice will rise. A new acquaintance and/or the revelation of a new facet in a current partner.

Better integration into one's life, in other words, into the querent's surroundings.

Reverse: Enslavement to the pursuit of the material realm (including physical sexuality) debases love, in the querent's view.

Queen. The capacity for powerful, focused love. Open, multifaceted sexuality. Extremes of love and hate. The desire to gather the family together under the wings of the Great Mother.

Reverse: A domineering "mother" is the prominent characteristic of the woman. Material overcomes spirit.

King. Pleasure from physical love, reaching pathological dimensions.

Hedonism - realistic and not exaggerated. Conservatism. A family in which the father is the central figure. At a later stage in life, love loses its attraction.

Reverse: An attempt to control others via sex. Using the material realm in order to attain selfish goals. Living for the sake of making an impression.

KNIGHT of PENTACLES

Prince. Difficulty in combining the love of the spiritual with the pursuit of the material.

The search for inner identity causes confusion.

A situation that is usually at the beginning stages, prior to selecting an objective.

A person (usually a young man) who thinks that by controlling material matters, he will reach "correct" love.

Reverse: A spiritual crisis. A gamble. Walking on the cutting edge of the sword. A deviation from the material boundaries of the querent (who takes upon himself more than his nature allows).

PAGE of PENTACLES.

Princess. Sensuality, romance tinged with the virginal and the pristine. Love is dazzling the couple.

A yearning for adventure within the framework of the search for inner identity.

Joy stemming from physical experiences. May also be an indication of motherhood (mainly in anticipation of or following a first birth).

Reverse: Disappointment with a spouse, particularly for a young woman. "Unmasking" - blind love opens its eyes, and the revelation destroys an old relationship.

Cups

1. A powerful lust for the erotic, the unusual and the exotic in physical love. Strong sexuality (including fertility). A full emotional life.

Each time a new love is uncovered, it is located at a higher level. Intuitive activity.

Reverse: A dangerous illusion in the realm of love.

2. Love energy dominates the querent (at the time of the spread). Strong eroticism. The querent is losing his head over love. Extremism and a great deal of centeredness. Positive use of love energy.

Reverse: A person who is emotionally closed, trying to force his world view on those around him. Crises. This card may also indicate sexual coercion on the part of one of the partners.

3. Pregnancy and birth. Harmony in personal relationships. A balanced emotional life leads to creativity. A baby symbolizes self-fulfillment. A couple who becomes a "threesome" of their own volition.

Reverse: An invasion of the couple's relationship causes a crisis that could lead to a break-up of the relationship.

4. An attempt to institutionalize love (by marriage, for example) in order to preserve it. Paving a new way based on love and mutual respect. A long-lasting connection based on good harmony and balance. A great intensity in love may serve as a catalyst for creativity or progress in life (especially when one of the partners is involved in art or other creative fields).

Reverse: A relationship that has lasted for too long, that lacks harmony and balance, is about to end. An attempt to create a perfect love based on imbalance and incompatibility is doomed to failure from the start.

5. Some (external) element is undermining the querent's love. He needs to alter his emotional attitude. This change must occur throughout all of his personal relationships. From a more positive perspective, this process will enrich and develop his emotional capacity.

Reverse: Crisis, disappointment with an emotional attitude directed towards the querent. A new perception of the partner is tying the emotional energy in painful knots. A lack of clarity is causing confusion.

6. Great satisfaction from erotic passion. Harmony in emotional energy (particularly as a result of mutual emotional honesty). Balance. An atmosphere of joy and happiness. Preferring *togetherness* to *individuality*.

Reverse: A danger of illusion, the pursuit of false magic - a trick. Action resulting from the wrong motive. A significant card, particularly in the case of young people.

7. The querent sees love as the central element in his life (and in everyone's lives, for that matter). Stormy emotions. A situation in which it is necessary for the querent to evaluate his emotions cautiously. An opportunity to develop new horizons in the emotional realm. Usually indicates the situation of someone who is the object of a strong love.

Reverse: Blind love. The querent is complicating his life by allowing himself to be bound by the bonds of love, while not knowing what he is up against. His life is being controlled by impulse.

8. Overflowing emotions. The querent seeks, locates and tastes the nectar of love with all his senses! A great deal of self-confidence. A long-lasting love with a potential for perfect harmony.

Reverse: An unproductive search for love. Alternatively, love that becomes dogmatic over time and loses its flexibility and freshness. In this situation, it is conceivable that energy barriers and crises will quickly put an end to this relationship.

9. Erotic fulfillment of the demands of love. A stage in which the querent is on a higher level of harmonious love. An opportunity to strengthen feelings of love. Great sensitivity. His "antennae" are receptive to love energy. (Note that in this situation, love relationships are formed rapidly... but also end just as quickly!)

Reverse: An emotional obstacle. The inability to open new channels of love towards a partner. An extreme reaction to this condition might lead to the erection of a cool and indifferent emotional barrier directed at the entire world.

10. *A perfect love in a joint consummation.* In other words, the querent compromises a bit in order to reach a higher level of love with his partner.

This is a crucial stage on the road to pure, supreme love. Mature love. Mutual nourishing via the energy of love.

Reverse: Great pressure in the querent's love life is creating fissures and crises. He wishes to fulfill himself in love, but is choosing the wrong way in which to do so.

QUEEN of CUPS.

Queen. Living by the emotions (by the heart). When a woman reveals this card, it indicates a high degree of sensuality and eroticism. In the case of a man, it indicates that the woman described here is the one he is yearning for!

Emotional life. Taking the expression of feelings to extremes. Love is the highest priority. A life based on intuition.

Reverse: Doubts, a lack of both self-confidence and personal honesty that is harmful to emotional life. Domination. A situation in which a woman relates to the whole world as if she were a mother hen and all the world her vulnerable chicks.

KING of CUPS.

King. Sensitivity coupled with great ambitiousness is a dangerous combination.

Regarding a woman, it speaks of the fulfillment of hidden sexuality. With reference to a man, it points to the use of sexuality to achieve his goals.

(However, this does not harm the strong energy of sex.)

This situation may frequently create dependence or patronage in a couple's relationship.

Reverse: A person without a backbone, motivated by cold logic - as a reaction to impulses and urges - working to attain selfish objectives. Hatred and jealousy are liable to blind love!

Prince. A subtle promise of a better love. For a woman, this card hints at a loving younger man as a partner. Regarding a man, this card clearly indicates that he must take some time to work on his feelings of love and on his ability to receive and accept love.

Reverse: Using love in order to achieve personal goals. "Fatal charm". Using sex and love in order to enslave others. Avoiding emotional commitment.

PAGE of CUPS.

Princess. Living by one's emotions. Primality with regard to the erotic realm. Longing for love (to give and take). Using sexuality, especially feminine sexuality, in order to attain an objective. A new relationship.

Reverse: An attempt to relive something lost and gone, to cling to the past instead of looking forward. Hypersensitivity leading to emotional crises. A tendency to manipulate in one's interpersonal relations.

Swords

1. A new love! This love may open up new channels of energy, not only in the emotional, but also in the intellectual realm. Illumination. Magnetic sexuality. Success. A sudden change during which new opportunities for personal development are revealed.

Reverse: Insufficient energy for coping with changes, new energies and a demanding partner. A disparity in expectations. Crises resulting from the age of the querent.

2. Tension as a result of a struggle between forces. Extremism. The state of balance is endangered. A situation of *duality*... anything can happen! Nevertheless, there is now an opportunity for discussing problems and finding solutions. Conflicting motives.

Reverse: Ignoring problems. A tough

struggle. Disregarding possible ways of solving problems.

3. Burning passion. Flowing energy is feeding the fires of love. Fertile cooperation. An important card in a spread because of its great intensity.

Reverse: Boredom in a relationship. A dangerous situation liable to undermine the foundations of loving harmony.

4. An established, quiet and stable life. Living according to an internal charter of love. Following the middle path prevents extremism. In this situation, the querent may be self-contained; in other words, he may avoid a relationship since he is "OK" with his own emotions. Seeking a relationship with another.

Reverse: An attempt to contain emotions within logic.... A dangerous and ineffective endeavor when it comes to a person's love life!

5. Sensuality... which withstands the test, in view of the fact that a new direction of action must be chosen. The querent is utilizing his faculties and senses to their fullest regarding emotions and love. An attempt to build a new relationship based on an existing relationship.

Reverse: Cracks... particularly in one's self-confidence. An existing relationship is being undermined. Exposure to crises.

6. The pursuit of pleasure... while also preserving harmony and balance. Sexual enjoyment. Self-confidence. Harmony within the family. Intense physical enjoyment. Great sexual power.

Reverse: Ignoring problems. Covering up problems instead of solving them by building a renewed relationship. Problems and crises can be expected in the future.

7. An unstable situation in the realm of love. Crisis. An abyss has opened up in the relationship. It is imperative to clarify things and reestablish the feelings of love. Only cooperation between partners and a lot of hard work will put love back on an even keel.

Reverse: A crisis that will lead to separation. A tough struggle. At times, violence, which destroys love life.

8. Love at first sight!

The querent is flooded with a love which is seeking expression. Strong energy. A change is necessary, although we do not yet know the direction of that change. One must not fall into stagnation... it is essential to be active, to search for a way, to initiate and to react.

Reverse: Ignoring problems will lead to crisis and separation. A person who is torn apart within by contradictory tendencies.

9. The querent is freeing himself from the bonds of a "rusty" relationship. Separation without much quarreling. Making way for a new relationship. Fear of a relationship in which love is the central element.

Reverse: Desperation. The querent hates himself and thereby neutralizes his ability to cope with his surroundings, particularly in the area of the emotions and love. A difficult situation that may lead to a genuine crisis.

10. Combined energies. The querent is acting in accordance with his personal karma, and is realizing his destiny. New energies in love. Fulfillment of aspirations. Blooming sexuality.

Reverse: Stagnation. It appears as if the flow of energy has become a weighty, burdensome mass pulling him down into the depths.

Queen. An extreme love, overwhelming.

A man who is attracted to women.

A woman who reveals her full sexuality.

Open sexuality, revealing, flaunted in public.

An externalization of sexuality to a great extent. Sexual energy coming in bursts.

It is difficult to predict what will happen to the person and how he will react in different situations.

Reverse: The querent is angry at himself and is serving as his own "lightning rod". A difficult situation, leading to personal crises that demand attention.

King. A determined pursuit of sex as a way to extinguish an inner fire.

In the case of a man, this condition might lead him to an exaggerated pursuit of women, to the point of being pathological.

In the case of a woman, it usually indicates a lack of satisfaction. A situation in which abstaining from logical thought causes the desired emotional direction to disappear.

Reverse: The querent's personal problems are also turning into external problems.

Violence. Outbursts.

Unexpected reactions (mainly negative ones).

KNIGHT of SWORDS.

Prince. Searching for love. Change.

If the subject is a woman, this card shows that a young, handsome man is awaiting her.

Regarding a man, it indicates the pursuit of his "fairy princess", who is only a fantasy.

A great deal of excitement in the realm of love life.

Reverse: A waste of energy. A lack of direction.

Indifference to sexuality.

PACE of SWORDS

Princess. Change, surprise. Sexual fantasies as a motivating force, aided by imagery.

Virginal sexuality (for a woman), true love (for a man). New content in life.

Reverse: A lack of satisfaction. The search for instant release, temporary and short-lived, rather than true love.

SPREADS FOR LOVE

The first and most important thing to remember about the Tarot of Love is that the usual rules governing the spread of cards in general also apply to spreads relating to love.

It is crucial that the cards be related to appropriately and shuffled correctly, that a Significator Card be chosen (if necessary) and that the proper spread be prepared.

Only after the cards are actually spread will we move into the interpretations according to the Tarot of Love.

These rules must be adhered to, no matter which deck you are using for a spread.

Although there is no difference in the way the spread is "technically" prepared, there is a difference between the spreads used in the Tarot of Love and other spreads.

When using the Tarot of Love, the reader must be much more relaxed, tranquil and "loving" than for other spreads.

It is crucial to make sure that the cards are spread in a quiet place in which the reader feels good. In addition, more time should be devoted to the spreads of the Tarot of Love than to regular spreads.

It is important to remember that the Tarot of Love actually involves three levels of interpretation or prediction:

The first level, presented in the 22 cards of the Major Arcana, relates to the basic energies (sometimes subconscious energies) which direct the querent and determine his talents and characteristics.

The second level, presented in the 16 court cards, relates to personal aspirations, past experiences and ego, as expressed in everyday life, as well as to the querent's talents as they actually manifest themselves.

The third level, which relates to the 40 *number* cards, expresses the transient, coincidental events which occur in each person's life.

SPECIAL CARDS

In addition, one must remember the principles of interpreting a spread. *Several cards (from the Major Arcana) have a special meaning within a spread,* and their significance is outstanding and unequivocal:

Card #6 indicates that the energies of love have been activated! This card also points to sexual "fulfillment".

Card #7 indicates energies of friendship (positive energies at a *very low* level).

Card #9 indicates that the individual is alone, *but not lonely*. The search for energies of friendship or love.

Card #10 indicates that the querent is in the hands of his fate and is not in control of his life.

Card #11 indicates sexual orgasm or, in a negative context, a difficult crisis in the querent's love life.

Card #12 indicates a situation urgently demanding a fundamental change in the querent's life.

Card #13 indicates a fundamental change. Some say this card describes "a transition from darkness to light... or a transition from light to darkness"!

Card #14 indicates harmony and a "whole and perfect" situation.

Card #15 indicates broadening, in other words, abilities, talents... or aspirations.

Card #16 indicates a sudden, severe crisis. This interpretation applies whether the card is upright or reversed. (However, when the card is upright, it points to the fact that the querent will overcome the crisis, and when the card is reversed, it indicates that he will be defeated by the crisis).

Card #17 indicates cosmic energies merging with the querent's own energies.

Card #21 indicates soul-mates, in other words, a person whose destiny is bound to the destiny of another, for good and for bad.

Card #0 (The Fool) is a reminder that one's life is only a small isolated point in the great cycle of creation!

And of course, in any case, each card must be considered within the context of its position in the spread, whether it is upright or reversed, and which cards are adjacent to it.

THE FIVE RECOMMENDED SPREADS
FOR THE TAROT OF LOVE

The Time-Line Spread

This spread teaches about the *consistent nature* of the flow of love energy in one's life.

It involves only three cards, placed from left to right. It is advisable to select the three cards after the deck has been cut, and the half that has been chosen has been spread like a fan in front of the querent. From this array, he then randomly chooses three cards.

Past   Present   Future

The left card indicates the past, what has accumulated in the querent's life regarding the active energy of love. If the card is reversed, it is a sign that he is dragging a heavy, negative burden behind him.

The middle card indicates the present, the manner in which the querent is actually, currently, coping with love. If the card is reversed, he is avoiding the struggle with the energy of love.

The right card indicates aspirations, impulses and desires in this realm. If the card is reversed, it is a sign that the querent feels confused and embarrassed in this realm.

The Star of Love Spread

This is the most popular spread for the Tarot of Love, and it utilizes a Significator Card (see the Infroduction for the rules for choosing this card) and five additional cards. The Significator Card is chosen from the deck *before it is shuffled.*

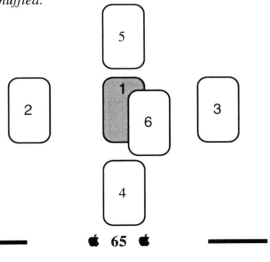

The Significator Card (#1) indicates a problem that the querent has. *This card must always be placed upright!*

The Card of Femininity (#2) indicates feminine energies (also found in every man).

The Card of Masculinity (#3) indicates masculine energies (also found in every woman).

The Card of Reincarnation (#4) indicates the querent's past, including earlier incarna- tions and the subconscious.

The Card of Hope (#5) indicates hopes and aspirations that shape the querent's future.

The Card of Challenge (#6) indicates the challenges the querent has to face and the forces that are available to him for this purpose (or that interfere with his facing the challenge).

In this spread, it is especially important to remember the remarks concerning the cards of the Major Arcana, discussed earlier.

The Spread of the Never-Ending Dialogue

This spread is actually an expansion of the usual spread used for an inquiry, and is executed only when *both partners* are present. In this spread, two Significator Cards are chosen from the deck, one for the woman and another for the man, and are placed at the head of each column (Card #1 is the woman's and Card #2 is the man's.)

2 Man	1 Woman
4	3
6	5
8	7

Then a question concerning the couple is asked, for example, "Should we marry?" After determining the question, the woman chooses a card and reveals it in her column (Card #3), and the man chooses a card and reveals it in his column (Card #4). When both cards are revealed, the question is answered *with regard to both cards together.*

Another question is asked, or a clarifying question is asked concerning the first question. Two additional cards are revealed in the same manner, and the second question is answered... and so on. One may continue in this manner, but it is not advisable to answer more than 11 consecutive questions (in other words, a spread of two columns containing 12 cards each, including the Significator Card).

The Celtic Spread for the Tarot of Love

This is a well-known spread which utilizes the most popular Tarot spread. Ten cards are used, placed consecutively in the familiar pattern.

Card #1 teaches about the problem or challenge the querent faces.

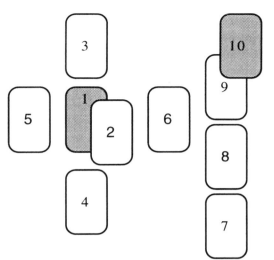

Card #2 speaks of the "loving" or supportive elements in the querent's path.

Card #3 teaches about the ability of the love relationship to develop.

Card #4 speaks of emotions and residues from the past.

Card #5 teaches about the trials and experiences the querent has undergone in the past, and which still influence him today.

Card #6 teaches about the energies that are acting upon the querent in the present (energies that are not his own!).

Card #7 teaches about the *general impression the reader has* of the querent.

Card #8 teaches about the way in which the "problem" or "challenge" found in Card #1 (usually a partner) reacts to the querent's energy.

Card #9 teaches about future challenges.

Card #10 teaches about a "closing" or "new beginnings" - in other words, what will develop at the basis of the querent's being as a result of the energies and elements which have acted, and continue to act, upon him.

The Loving Stars Spread

A simple application of the regular astrological-Tarot spread. Twelve cards are used, placed according to the order of the horoscope, with each sign representing a realm or house. The order of the spread is preserved in the accompanying diagram (Aries being the card on the far left in the circle). However, the cards are placed counter-clockwise beginning with the querent's sun sign.

In other words, if the querent is a Gemini, the first card chosen will be placed in the position of Card #3, the second card will be placed on Cancer, Card #4... etc., until the last card, the twelfth in the series, which will be placed in the position of Card #2, Taurus.

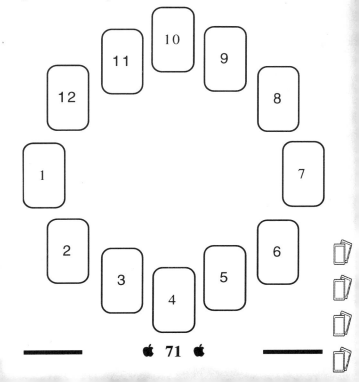

Pay close attention to this rule!

Card #1 - Aries: Relationship with a spouse.

Card #2 - Taurus: "Material", from physical to monetary.

Card #3 - Gemini: Communication, sharing.

Card #4 - Cancer: Residue from the past in the conscious and in the subconscious.

Card #5 - Leo: "windows of opportunity" or possibilities that are open to the querent.

Card #6 - Virgo: A couple relationship. The most important card in this spread!

Card #7 - Libra: Expectations from a partner.

Card #8 - Scorpio: Crises, and the ability to overcome them.

Card #9 - Sagittarius: "Spirit", from awareness to illumination (parallel to Card #2).

Card #10 - Capricorn: The ability to overcome, repair and uplift the relationship.

Card #11 - Aquarius: Aspirations and inhibitions, particularly in the realm of the subconscious.

Card #12 - Pisces: The spiral of the development of love or the ability of a person to "love more".